"Some books on anxiety make you feel the author really gets anxiety. Others offer clear and helpful solutions. *Hope in an Anxious World* does both. Simple, clear and accessible, this book reorients us in our anxiety with highly practical advice, showing what we can learn from psychology's experience and then majoring on the deep wellsprings of help and hope found in the Scriptures."

J. ALASDAIR GROVES, Executive Director, CCEF

"This book is packed full of understanding and encourage-ment for our battle with anxiety. It not only takes the best self-help strategies but goes further by addressing the lies that lurk behind anxiety and by helping us to hear what God says in response. It is accessible and engaging for both Christians and others who are willing to see what wisdom the Bible has for addressing anxiety. It is a book that I will be returning to myself, and I will be recommending it to all those who struggle with anxieties—big and small."

DR JOANNA JACKSON, Director of Counselling,
All Souls Counselling Service

"Helen Thorne has provided a concise and helpful guide to managing your anxiety. As a struggler herself, she wisely pays attention to both body and soul while being a compas-sionate voice that you will relate to. Practical techniques coupled with a strong Redeemer are just what we need and what she offers."

DR TIM LANE, President, Institute for Pastoral Care

"Those struggling with anxiety need a resource that is short, relatable... and actually useful. Helen has delivered this and more. I appreciate her realistic perspective and rich teaching: though our anxiety may be a daily battle, we do not fight alone but in the strength that God supplies and with his ever-present help. Highly recommend this!"

KRISTEN WETHERELL, Author, *Fight Your Fears*

"In the disorienting swirl of anxious thoughts and feelings, we need simple, clear and reassuring truth. Helen manages to capture the experience of fear in tangible descriptions, to help us understand its causes and, most importantly, to bring gospel realities to bear on our struggles. But perhaps we are most indebted to Helen for speaking personally out of lived experience. When she says there is hope, we listen. When she shares what helps, we benefit. And as she does all this, she comforts us with the comfort of God. I benefitted from reading this, and as a counsellor I expect to be recommending it over and over."

DR ANDREW COLLINS, Consultant Psychiatrist
and Biblical Counsellor

"This warm, grace-filled, sympathetic book will be a help to many. Helen Thorne sits at the reader's side and walks them gently through wonderful Bible truth. The book is earthed in experience, informed by counselling skills and written in an easy-to-read style. I recommend it warmly."

CHRISTOPHER ASH, Writer-in-Residence,
Tyndale House, Cambridge

"The events of 2020 have only exacerbated the epidemic of anxiety sweeping through our society. Teenagers, children and adults alike are susceptible to its powerful—and deeply damaging—lies. Helen Thorne speaks powerfully from her personal experience of anxiety and of the hope that counteracts those lies. This book doesn't offer the false hope of a miraculous cure but something far better—the true hope that is found in Christ, who walks with us, shares our burdens, and leads us into a place of confidence and joy."

ROS CLARKE, Associate Director, Church Society

HELEN THORNE

HOPE

IN AN

ANXIOUS

WORLD

thegoodbook
COMPANY

Hope In an Anxious World
© Helen Thorne, 2021. Reprinted 2021.

Published by
The Good Book Company

thegoodbook.com | thegoodbook.co.uk
thegoodbook.com.au | thegoodbook.co.nz | thegoodbook.co.in

Unless indicated, all Scripture references are taken from the Holy Bible, New International Version. Copyright © 2011 Biblica, Inc. Used by permission.

ISBN: 9781784986261 | Printed in Denmark

Design by André Parker

CONTENTS

INTRODUCTION

Do you ever dream about life being different?

Have you ever longed to get through a day without second-guessing yourself or poring over regrets? Do you sometimes wonder what it would be like to have no more sweaty palms, palpitations or panic? Maybe you picture yourself being able to fall asleep, confident that you won't be waking up with a start or melting down the next day. Perhaps you long for a time when you don't feel overwhelmed or don't want to run away anymore.

Such dreams are beautiful. They're places where you can flourish—moments when the struggles fade away. But if you are anything like me, you aren't living the dream. Maybe you can't even begin to believe the dream could ever come true! You're hurting—or you know someone who is.

Whether mild, moderate or severe, anxiety is a struggle many of us know well. At its core, it's a fear: a sense of worry or tension about what is or what might

occur. But it's not one that helps. Some fear is useful—
an awareness of danger is necessary to help us keep
safe—but anxiety is a type of fear that is persistent,
difficult to control and detrimental to life. It drags us
down, it stops us thriving, it leaves us unequipped for
the day ahead.

There are valid reasons why we struggle. It is under-
standable that sometimes anxiety grips our heart. But
staying trapped is not inevitable. There is wisdom in
the world around us and hope from the heavens above
us. At least some of those dreams for a new way of being
can really come true.

In what follows, we're going to go on a journey together:
one that helps us understand anxiety better, learn some
useful techniques and, most importantly, hear from the
living God, who has some astonishingly precious things
to say to our hurting hearts.

It may be that you are used to reading about God—he's
central to your life, and you're keen to hear his words.
If so, what follows is likely to contain some familiar
verses but ones that maybe you've never applied to
your anxiety before. But perhaps you aren't sure if God
really exists or if he cares about your anxiety in any
meaningful way. If that's you, much of what follows
may be new. It will be a chance to look at the Bible and,
in the process, look at the world from God's perspective
and see the difference he can make to every anxious

heart. Whichever you are, I hope you'll read on. This book is designed to have words of encouragement for everyone who struggles with anxiety (and that's most of us to a greater or lesser extent). As you read, it is my prayer that you will come to see real hope and take the first few steps in a lifetime of change.

PART ONE

AN

ANXIOUS

WORLD

1. LIVING
THE DREAM?

"Anxiety is a feeling of unease, such as worry or fear, that can be mild or severe.

"Everyone has feelings of anxiety at some point in their life. For example, you may feel worried and anxious about sitting an exam, or having a medical test or job interview.

"During times like these, feeling anxious can be perfectly normal.

"But some people find it hard to control their worries. Their feelings of anxiety are more constant and can often affect their daily lives." [1]

No two people's experience of anxiety is exactly the same.

Some of us will be wrestling with anxiety that's linked to a specific event in the near future: a set of exams, an interview or an important presentation can all elicit a few weeks of pain.

Others of us will be aware of the tension that arises from not knowing how a longer-term circumstance might turn out. A cancer diagnosis, the choices being made by a teenage child, a difficult intimate relationship (or the absence of any intimate relationship at all), an elderly parent who needs increasing care or the impact of unemployment on finances and home—all these can impact our wellbeing and nudge us to worry for weeks or years.

At other times our anxiety is far less linked to objective events. It can be a nebulous sense that life isn't safe, that there's something bad out there, or maybe a sneaking suspicion that we might be the something bad ourselves. Life, in all its aspects, can feel like a threat, a pressure or a heavy burden to bear.

For many, anxiety is mostly low level. It ebbs and flows. If this is you, you may never have thought of going to the doctor about it—you just grit your teeth and wish it would go away. For those who have seen a doctor, there are further nuances in the different diagnoses. Some will have been told they have a generalised anxiety disorder—a sense of dis-ease that spans six months or more. The anxiety of others may be focused on some specific aspects of meeting other people (social anxiety disorder), difficulties related to leaving the home (agoraphobia) or fears for personal ill-health (health anxiety disorder). There are those whose anxiety is rooted in deeply disturbing events from the past (post-traumatic stress disorder) or where panic attacks are the dominant trait (panic disorder). There are many more descriptors than these in the world of psychiatry. Even within those medical classifications, there are stories that show that anxiety is not one-size-fits-all.

But we probably all recognise some of the common physical signs: restlessness, fatigue, palpitations and sweats are just some of the body's ways of showing us it's not ok. Eating can be a chore, sleeping an impossible goal. Tension in the shoulders can build up to the point where even raising an arm can bring yelps of pain. At its most serious, blood pressure rises and ulcers develop, which can cause serious physical harm. For all, anxiety is felt deeply in our flesh.

It's not just physical, though. There are emotional symptoms too: the tears, the panic, the sense of overwhelming doom. There can be fear, hyper-vigilance or a sense that life will never again be fine. Minds can become obsessed with turning over past events or catastrophising what might come. It can feel impossible to believe that something might just work out or that we have what it takes to cope. A sense of self-despair often permeates each day. Or a feeling of exasperation with ourselves: why on earth can't I cope better than this?

Relationally too, anxiety can take a desperate toll. The desire to withdraw from loved ones can be so very strong, it becomes a survival strategy to those in pain. It's hard to return calls, turn up at events or believe that anyone could truly care. Misunderstandings abound. Friendships stumble and fail. And it doesn't stop there. The irritability and anger that flow from never feeling safe can wound others to the core. We might long for intimacy one day and flee from it the next. Family and friends can be left confused and hurt by the one they are committed to standing alongside. Sometimes we convince ourselves that people would be better off without us. "Maybe I should leave," we quietly muse.

And, for many, spiritual questions—big questions—weigh heavily on our hearts. Is there anyone out there or am I on my own in this? If there is a God, why would he let me languish in this level of pain? Surely, if he loved me, he'd want to make it right? Am I failing God in some way for feeling like this? Am I being punished for something bad I've done?

Different struggles, one goal

So much varies, but one thing is common to all: we hate feeling anxious day by day. Those signs and symptoms we've been listing above might be as familiar as an old pair of shoes, but they make life hard, and many of us would try anything to get the feelings to go away. If we're honest, some of us have tried things we know aren't wise—even things that actually tend to make our anxiety worse in the end. A quiet drink, just to steel the nerves. A purchase we can't quite afford, kidding ourselves that retail therapy might actually help. A little more medication than the doctor prescribed. Avoiding preparations for an important meeting in the hope it might not happen. A dive into an online game so all-consuming that we barely even remember our problems anymore. Time lingering on a website or book that isn't wholesome or wise—one that fuels a fantasy that is far more alluring than the life we lead... The details vary from person to person, but the goal is common to nearly everyone who reels. We want to escape. We want to leave anxiety far behind. We long to be something—someone—else. And while those feelings may be strong, many of us are too ashamed to even acknowledge they're there.

If any of that sounds familiar, you are not alone. Around 6% of the UK population will seek medical help for anxiety in any given year.[2] As many as 1 in 3 in the West will struggle at some point in their life. It impacts the young and the old, the high-flying professional and the housebound alike; it blights those with an abundance of qualifications and those with none; it is no respecter of ethnicity, cultural background or family history. If you are struggling, please hear this loud and clear: you are not odd or weird or out on your own.

You're not stuck either.

I've battled anxiety for much of my life, and I've walked alongside many others who have too. I know what it's like to have a head that feels as if it is exploding with pressure, to want to run and hide. I understand what it is to be tempted to dive into all kinds of unhelpful coping mechanisms that help me forget the world and enjoy a few fleeting moments of calm. It hurts—it's horrible. I get it, truly I do.

But as well as tasting the pain, I've tasted change too. I'm not as anxious as I used to be, not by a mile. Nor are many of the people I've counselled over the years. We've grown—day by day we've been transformed— to be more trusting, more confident, more convinced of what the Bible says is true.

I'll be honest, there's no quick fix for anxiety or guarantee of a completely worry-free life in the years to come. But there is hope of something better. A hope of a life where anxiety doesn't rule each day. A life where we can, step by step, move away from our fears and begin to thrive, maybe for the first time in years.

2. LIVING IN THE REAL WORLD

It wasn't supposed to be this way. When the world first came into being, it was intended to be a place where we all could thrive. If we flick to the beginning of the Bible, we can see that God designed a perfect world, an ordered world: one where there was no sickness, pain or fear. Humans had an intimate relationship with God, unswervingly peaceful interactions with each other and work that was always fulfilling and stress-free.

The good news is that, one day, there will be a future when it's like that again. God has promised that there will come a time when everything is restored to how it should be—how it was designed to be right at the start. No more arguments or uncertainty, no abuse or prejudice, no more illness of any kind—not a hint of anxiety to be found. Maybe you call it "the afterlife"; the Bible terms it "the new heavens and the new earth". Whichever, it's coming, and the end of the book of Revelation paints a beautiful picture of just how wonderful it will be.

> *Look! God's dwelling-place is now among the people, and he will dwell with them. They will be his people, and God himself will be with them and be their God. "He will wipe every tear from their eyes. There will be no more death" or mourning or crying or pain, for the old order of things has passed away.* (Revelation 21 v 3-4)

That is what God promises to those who would follow him into the life to come.

But we don't live at the start or at the end of the Bible story. Not yet. We are in the middle, facing the brokenness and pain of the world as it is now, waiting for God to finish what he has started, waiting for perfection to return.

This is a life where there are three major reasons why anxiety abounds.

Broken experiences

The Bible tells us that the problems all began in a garden—the garden of Eden, to be precise. There, the first humans had an incredible life, perfect in every way. They had the freedom to do anything they liked, except eat the special fruit of one specific tree. You might think that sounds like a good deal, but Adam and Eve clearly didn't agree. After being tempted by the devil, they became discontent with this "limit" on their lives. Why couldn't they eat this fruit? Why couldn't they benefit from the wisdom and power it would bring? As they looked at the fruit, they began to want it more and more. They wanted to live life God's way less and less.

Eve took the first bite. Adam followed swiftly on. For a moment it tasted good, but then the enormity of their actions began to kick in. They had done the one thing they had been told not to do. They had disobeyed the one who loved them best. So they hid from God. They blamed each other. They sacrificed life in the garden for a momentary mouthful. And nothing has been perfect since.

It's this story that helps us understand why we so often experience discord with those around us and a disconnect from the very world in which we live. We have a broken relationship with God. We aren't at peace with each other. We are no longer living the life we were designed to live. You can feel it day by day— that sense that everything is not as it should be.

We all of us know the reality of that tension, to a greater or lesser extent. All of us have been on the receiving end of words or actions that have brought deep pain. All of us have said or done things that are far from what God would wish and, in the process, have caused hurt to those around us. That means we all have things that we look back on with shame; every one of us carries at least one scar from the past, and probably more. Each individual can look around, in the present, and see things in their lives that are not as they should be. There are reasons why we are scared of the future: it is full of other people, and we don't know how they are going to behave.

Life hurts. The past, the present and the future are all broken—fallen, to use the Bible word—and each aspect of that fallenness nudges us towards anxiety. The abuse, the bullying, the rejection, the arguments, the loneliness, the exhaustion and grief—it all piles on and shouts in our ear, "This world is not safe; you have reason to fear". It's no wonder we get anxious. We are not unaffected by the things that come at us day by day.

Broken bodies
It's not just the stuff coming at us that hurts, though. Our very bodies can fail us at every turn. Some of us are generally healthy, while others are facing our last few months, but for all there is a struggle. We know what it is for our bodies to simply not function well.

If we are unwell, we can be all the more fearful of the future. Will my condition be easily treatable or will it limit my life in some way? We might be worried about the treatment: will it hurt, will I cope with the isolation, will the side effects feel even worse than the underlying problem did? If it's really serious, maybe we're asking whether we will get through. All of us have to face the reality of our mortality at some stage. Even if we recover fully, the nagging worries can persist: maybe it'll return, maybe I'll pass it on to my children, maybe there will be complications—it happens, after all.

There is also another way in which anxiety can be related to our physical being. It can itself have deep roots in our biological form. For example, changes in our hormones can bring a biochemically induced sense of dread. For some that is a persistent feeling, for others a regular cycle where specific days result in tears and anger that don't quite fit with what's actually going on in the world around us. Similarly, genetic predispositions to anxiety may, perhaps, be connected to particular tendencies in our neurochemistry. More serious—but much rarer—are conditions like brain tumours, which can alter our very perception of life.

As human beings we are both body and soul. We have an outer fleshly bit and an inner core where we feel, think and decide how to respond—and those two aspects of our lives are deeply connected. It's not just what's going on in our minds that matters; what happens in our bodies matters too. Our biochemistry impacts us and, for some at least, there is a strong physiological driver to the anxiety we feel day by day.

That's why it's important to get a medical perspective on our anxiety. Doctors are people who understand the body well. And that's why churches care for people in practical ways, not just spiritual ones. Both the inner and the outer facets of our lives matter deeply to God.

Broken hearts

When it comes to anxiety, however, there is another factor that is often overlooked. It's not just the things that come at us in life or even just the things that go wrong in us that cause our anxiety to form and flare; there are also desires coming out of us, and they can rock us to the core.

Desires are not necessarily wrong. Of course, it's not good to want to dominate or control, to manipulate or destroy—those desires are clearly not what most of us want to be known for, nor are they what God would wish to see in us—but other desires are far kinder. It's good to want a spouse or children, to want to do well in our chosen career; it's normal to want to be healthy or to seek to enjoy the life we have here on earth. Trouble is, those desires can get out of control. We can tell God that if we don't have a certain spouse by a certain time, life won't be worth living. We can pretend that in order to get the job we want, we regularly need to work a 90-hour week, no rest. We can turn our desire for enjoyment into a demand for travel that puts us into debt and takes us away from family and friends. We can kid ourselves that to fit in and have friends, we need to drink to excess, engage in crime or take other unnecessary risks. Or that our houses have to be pristine if we are to have any peace in our minds. Those are good desires gone wrong: over-desires that drive us to pursue something at the expense of wisdom and love—and at the expense of our relationship with the one who sustains us every moment of every day.

Sometimes, we are anxious not because of tough things coming at us or hard things happening in our bodies but because we are pursuing things that just aren't wise. We can become relentless in our drive to obtain things which we do not need and which God has never promised. Disappointment and despair soon follow on. We spin a web of stress and get caught in our own trap.

Living in such a world, it's no wonder we struggle. No wonder that many have put time and effort into coming up with solutions—or coping strategies, at least. But what are those coping strategies? And, are they enough? In the next two chapters I want to look a little more closely at them and ask: What is good and helpful about the wisdom of the world around us? Is there any point in looking *beyond* what the self-help books say? And, if so, what words does the Bible say to the anxious at heart?

3. LIVING DAY
BY DAY

There are plenty of strategies to help keep symptoms at bay. Medics, psychologists, counsellors, and self-help gurus alike have all put time and effort into coming up with strategies to help us cope. Many of their ideas are worth enacting as we battle anxiety day by day.

Breathing and grounding

There are physical ways you can help your body become calm. The more anxious we get, the more shallow our breathing tends to become. Actively reversing that trend by taking slow deep breaths can bring a sense of peace. You can try breathing in slowly through your nose and out through your mouth, making sure your diaphragm moves smoothly as you go. Such breathing techniques can be used reactively, to combat anxiety that's already hit. But you can use them proactively too—perhaps at the start of each day taking a moment to focus on breathing in and out. Doing so is a practical way to head off anxiety before it arrives.

Grounding techniques can also be hugely useful, especially when a sense of panic begins to grow. As your heart rate rises, your chest tightens and your thoughts begin to spiral out of control, the whole of your being can be caught up in worries about what might come to pass. Bringing yourself back to the present—reminding yourself that you are safe in the here-and-now—is an essential skill to learn. One excellent example of a grounding technique is to survey your surroundings, looking for five things you can see, four things you can touch, three things you can hear, two things you can smell and one thing you can taste. Another is to use the top of your thumb to touch each of your fingertips in turn. The point is to give your body the physical stimulus it needs to be more aware of the now and focus less on what might be.

Exercise and rest

Some of us are natural gazelles while others of us seem to share more in common with the average sloth, but all of us need exercise if our bodies and minds are to work well. Whether it's a marathon run, a brisk walk around the local park or ten minutes of armchair exercises in whatever space you have in your room, there is much you can do to keep your body fit. Exercise releases endorphins, chemicals which have a positive impact on our mental health; it works the muscles that can tense up with stress; and it might even bring us face to face with people who make us smile! It is important to engage in activities that can give you the energy you need to face the tasks that come your way. Exercise can genuinely help keep anxiety at bay.

We aren't, however, designed to be people who are constantly on the go. If you're never sitting down, there is something seriously out of kilter in your life! Just as exercise is important, so rest has a vital part to play. God wasn't joking when he said that humans are designed for six days of work and one day of rest in any given week: day by day, sleep is a precious gift! If we constantly flout that plan and push ourselves at a relentless pace, it's bound to take its toll. If, on the other hand, we pursue regular rest, we will take a step closer to life as it should be. That doesn't mean complete inertia for a day, but you can make deliberate choices to put the to-do list to one side and do things like quietening yourself and thinking of your Maker, or engaging in a favourite activity, or meeting people who bring you joy.

Priorities and plans

Of course, it's not just taking a day off that counts; it's how we spend the other six days of the week too. If we set ourselves the task of pursuing the unobtainable—in our work, our parenting, our friendships, our hobbies or any other aspect of life—we are setting ourselves up to fail. We do not have the capacity to be perfect (not in this life). Contrary to what social media might suggest, most of us don't have the ability to be a model parent while simultaneously looking glamorous, holding down a responsible job, being at the forefront of social change, remaining at the peak of physical fitness and living in a flawless home. All of us will need to leave things undone, accept that we are limited and, at times at least, own the fact that we look as if we have been pulled through a bush backwards. If you are willing to try that, it will be a liberating choice.

It's a choice you will need to make deliberately, though. Changing our expectations, priorities and plans won't just automatically take place. You may need to step back from an activity, put in boundaries with your boss or friends, or review how many hobbies you expect or allow your children to undertake. (Overscheduling them is likely to produce anxiety in them and you!) You can opt to ignore the ironing (really, nothing bad happens—I've tried!) or accept a smaller house (who needs the extra dusting anyway?) or be content with non-designer trainers or tech. The decisions will look different for each of us, but there will certainly be choices to be made as we work to keep anxiety under control.

I've always been impressed by a decision my friend Ben made. In the same week, he was offered a promotion at work and discovered his wife was pregnant. Both bits of news filled him with delight! And, with a new baby on the way, the extra pennies would certainly come in handy. But he was already struggling with anxiety. He knew there would be inevitable sleepless nights ahead, and he doubted he would be able to cope. So he decided not to take the promotion—not there and then. He was open and honest with his boss—who reflected that his own marriage might have survived had he made that kind of decision in the past. And Ben stayed put. Not necessarily for ever—he might accept a promotion in the future—but for now.

Just as we deprioritise some things, so we might make other things a higher priority. Healthy eating might be one. Our bodies simply don't function properly without the right fuel. That might mean fewer takeaways, less junk and less alcohol, for a start. As my doctor always reminds me, your dinner plate should be full of natural colour!

Other things we will simply need to plan. It's not helpful to have general to-do lists where we dump everything (because they tend to get terrifyingly long and overwhelming!) or to just list what needs doing today (because we can easily lose the big picture); but dividing tasks into what needs doing today, next week and next month can be very useful indeed. Alternatively, you could try a year-planner that slots in tasks, not just meetings. This chapter was scheduled for a Monday morning in July—and most of it happened then!

Medication and talking therapies

Another wise strategy when faced with anxiety is to see the family doctor. There is no shame in accepting medication when it's required; we all need a prescription for something from time to time. Medics are best placed to look at the biochemical aspects of our anxiety—they know the human body better than you or me—and so it makes sense to allow them to diagnose underlying causes that stem from our flesh. And they can refer us on.

Skilled therapists can be a source of great help and hope. Wise men and women who can listen, ask perceptive questions and help us work out where we are thinking unhelpful thoughts and running to unhelpful strategies can be an enormous blessing. Counsellors and psychologists can help us respond to external and internal stimuli in far more healthy ways. They can enable us to make links between past experiences and present reactions. They can walk with us into the future and help us find new ways of coping with the very real stresses of life. If you need help from such professionals, please do seek it.

Is that it?

The reality, however, is that none of those things change our hearts. Resting, running, reprioritising and receiving the wisdom of those whose training far outweighs our own—plus all the rest of the techniques and ideas I've briefly outlined—are all good things to do, but we are still largely the same underneath. Take Ben, the man who temporarily passed up a promotion. Making that choice helped—it was undoubtedly the right thing for him and it helped keep some of the excesses of his anxiety at bay, but he was still a worrier at heart.

So what hope is there, at that deeper level?

Could there be something that might genuinely change our hearts?

4. LIVING
FOR MORE

Let me introduce you to one of my favourite women in the world. I've actually never met her—and don't even know her name—but I've read her story countless times.[3] She lived about 2,000 years ago in an area known as Samaria (in modern-day Palestine) and was pretty much an outcast in her town.

She was a woman—which, in a patriarchal society, meant she had few rights. She was a Samaritan—someone from a race that was frequently shunned by those around and of a religion that had taken just parts of the Bible and skewed what it said. And she had a reputation: she'd already had five husbands and was now living with another man.

Her life wasn't easy. She would have had plenty of reasons to struggle in all kinds of ways. To be honest, she was also the kind of person whom most religious leaders of the day would have avoided like the plague.

However, there was one religious leader who made a point of stopping and having a chat. When Jesus saw her approaching a well in the middle of the day, he asked the woman for a drink. It was a bit of a shock—and trampled over loads of cultural expectations—but the conversation progressed in intriguing ways.

Jesus showed that he knew her intimately, even though they had never met before. And as they conversed, he gradually helped her to get to know him in return. He described himself as the giver of "living water"—the person, the God, who can truly satisfy human beings on a deep level, both in the here-and-now and on into eternity. Not just the bringer of a religion but someone who helps people worship "in Spirit and in truth"—that is, to have a real relationship with the one true God. He said he was the "Christ" (God's King, promised in the Old Testament), who would reconcile people to the one who rules the universe. All in all, some pretty extraordinary claims!

This was no regular conversation, and it's no surprise that it had a major impact on the woman's life. After she'd finished speaking with Jesus, this outcast woman went door to door round her town and encouraged loads of people—people who would have shunned her in the past—to come and meet this incredible man. One meeting with Jesus and this woman went from being distant from God to being close; she went from being on the edge of her community to playing a pivotal role. And that made the world of difference to her life.

Why tell that story? Because it's a little picture of what God offers us all: an opportunity for messy people to discover who Jesus truly is, to follow him and, in the process, to have our lives transformed.

False hope

In a book on anxiety, it might be a nice sell if I could write, "Follow Jesus and your anxiety will instantly disappear". It probably won't. There are some highly dubious preachers who might peddle that line, and it can be tempting to believe their alluring words, but there are millions of Christians struggling with anxiety. We can all attest to the fact that having faith is no quick fix to life's pain.

Even some of the great heroes of the Bible struggled with fear. One Old Testament poet wrote a song which included the line, "When anxiety was great within me".[4] The people in the early church—those who had met Jesus or started following Jesus soon after his death and resurrection—struggled with worry, too. Paul, a wonderful church leader whose words are recorded in the New Testament, wrote a letter asking a church to arrange for his friend to come home. Why? So the church would be happy and he (Paul) would "have less anxiety".[5] Peter—one of the very first church leaders—encouraged his fellow-Christians to "cast all your anxiety on [God] because he cares for you".[6] Anxiety is normal in the Christian life. And faith is no protective bubble that insulates you from the pain.

So why talk about it in relation to anxiety at all? Shouldn't we just leave topics like this to psychiatrists, psychologists and others who are trained to help?

Real hope

Scripture is not a self-help book; its main purpose is not to make us feel better, and it speaks about far more than just our battles with fear. But in the midst of our anxiety, its words do give us hope. And they do so by pointing us to that same Jesus whom the Samaritan woman met—the one who can give us the new start, the new perspective and the new power we need.

God is not a remote, impersonal force but deeply involved in his world. He knows what's hurting and what's wrong; he cares about the way we have both received great pain and, at times, caused it in the lives of others; he gets that our relationships are not as they should be; he understands where our bodies are broken; and, most importantly, he has a plan to make things new.

Excitingly, he invites us to be part of that plan and to come with him on a journey—step by step—towards wholeness, towards being the kind of person that he originally designed us to be.

It's a journey I've been on for over 30 years. When I first started following Jesus, aged 20, I was anxious in the extreme. To be honest, I'd spent most of my life being scared of something or someone. Even as a child I wasn't the sort of person who felt confident to go out to play. But, gradually, as the journey has gone on, many of those fears have ebbed away. I'm no longer scared to speak in public, and I don't lie awake at night replaying the day anymore. It's even vaguely possible to sit next to me on a plane without me grabbing your arm. And that's not just because I've got older but because God has been at work—through his word, through his Holy Spirit, and through the encouragement of other believers.

I'm not anxiety-free yet. I am still quite capable of a headless-chicken routine! But I'm on the way, and God isn't going to stop working in me now. His invitation to journey is open to you too.

What next?

There are many ways a book like this could continue from here. We could look at aspects of God's character to see more of what he's like, or simply look up all the occurrences of the words "fear" and "anxiety" in the Bible and see what those passages have to say. We could look at different characters from the Bible and hear how God worked in their lives. We could share stories from the 21st century about how Christians battle anxiety day by day. Other books take more of those kinds of approaches, and many of them are definitely worth a read. (There are some ideas at the end of this book.) But in the chapters that follow, what we are going to do is consider some of the lies that our anxiety encourages us to believe, and hear what God has to say in response.

If you are anything like me, you can convince yourself that you are alone in your pain—that noone will ever truly understand the depths of the sorrows and fears that you bear. But it's a lie.

Like me, maybe you sometimes sit paralysed on your bed, utterly persuaded that your life is spiralling out of control—like a nightmare from which there seems to be no opportunity to wake. Or maybe you believe you are at sea, without the help needed to navigate this world's confusing and fear-inducing paths. More lies.

It doesn't end there. In your anxiety, do you hear the accusation that you are too weak, too exhausted, to engage with anything or anyone around? Or do you believe that you are guilty—so unendingly guilty—that noone would want to help? It isn't true.

Perhaps the biggest lie is that there is no hope for someone like you. You're too broken, too messed up, too worthless for anyone to want to get alongside you and enable you to change. But nothing could be further from the truth.

God wants us to know something better than these lies. He wants us to know someone—himself—who can lead us through the maze to a place of safety. And he wants us to know that, if we follow him and gradually replace those false beliefs with the deeply relational truths of the Bible, we can see our struggles with anxiety beginning to change. They may not disappear overnight, but they will definitely start to loosen their grip.

So let's look at the lies one by one and see what God has to say.

PART TWO

HOPE IN THE FACE OF ANXIETY'S LIES

5. LIE #1: I'M ALL ALONE

Anxiety is a lonely place. A cursory glance at our social-media feeds and everyone else appears to have it all. Their photos show them having fun with friends, and their status updates are an unending celebration of places they've been. It all looks so rosy and carefree. So very far from how we know our lives to be.

Even when we remind ourselves that social media isn't an accurate representation of how life is, that sense of being alone with our pain can remain. It's not just that our lives aren't quite as shiny as we might like them to be, but that we genuinely believe there is no one who gets us, no one who sees us as we truly are. Do you sometimes wonder if it's actually possible to find anyone who really understands how you feel? Others might have had some experience of worry, but it never quite seems the same as yours. And in the absence of any kind of sci-fi mind-meld that would enable us to show them the full scope of our broken thoughts, we can despair of ever finding someone who truly gets what we're going through.

Of course, some of us don't want people to know our thoughts; some of us have chosen not to tell anyone at all. Perhaps you're convinced there's noone who cares. Perhaps people feel scary. Perhaps you've tried to tell someone in the past, and it didn't go well. Sadly, I've known a few people who have assumed that, when it comes to anxiety, I should just be able to snap out of it. Maybe you, too, have come across people who make cutting comments that wound to the core. Ever been called "attention seeking"? Or accused of "making a scene"? It's no surprise if, when we've had our feelings trampled on once—or multiple times—we resolve never to go there again.

And so, when our anxious mind whispers, "You're all alone in this", we believe it. We can genuinely feel we will always be unknown, unloved and unsupported.

Alone is not how human beings are designed to be. We are relational creatures. Made to be known and loved. When God made the first human being, he made the man to be in relationship with himself. But that wasn't the only relationship needed. God said, "It is not good for the man to be alone" and made another human being—a complementary human being called Eve, who was equal but different—so that the two of them could be together, share together and enjoy life in God's world together.[7] That's why friends and family—when relationships are right—are such a blessing. That's why when relationships are broken, they cause such pain. That's the reason why solitary confinement is such an awful punishment and lockdown in a pandemic is a heavy burden to bear. Human beings are not islands. We are not designed to function by ourselves.

The Bible has good news, though. We are never alone.

In the middle of Scripture, there is a beautiful book of songs—Psalms—that help us speak to God and hear from him too. One psalm in particular reminds us that, even on our bleakest days, we can grasp a wonderful truth: God knows, and he cares.

It starts like this:

> *You have searched me, LORD,*
> *and you know me.*
> *You know when I sit and when I rise;*
> *you perceive my thoughts from afar.*
> *You discern my going out and my lying down;*
> *you are familiar with all my ways.*
> *Before a word is on my tongue*
> *you, LORD, know it completely.*
> *You hem me in behind and before,*
> *and you lay your hand upon me.*
> *Such knowledge is too wonderful for me,*
> *too lofty for me to attain.*   *(Psalm 139 v 1-6)*

It's an astonishing set of words: one that reminds us that even though God is huge and powerful, ruling over the entire universe and beyond, he is intimately involved in the lives of individual, messy human beings. He's the kind of God who isn't just interested in keeping planets spinning—he's also interested in you and every facet of your life.

Far from your struggles being played out in secret, away from the gaze of anyone who understands, there is one who is familiar with every single thought that has ever crossed your mind. One who knows every action that you have taken—and every event that has impacted you for good or ill. His understanding of you is so comprehensive that he even knows what you're going to say before you say it. You couldn't be more known!

And the God who knows is good and safe. This isn't some malicious cosmic surveillance system by which God monitors humans for information to store away in a heavenly supercomputer in order to manipulate or wound. He's not that kind of God! Of course, as he looks at our lives, he will see things that don't please him—not one of us has lived a life of perfection—but he's not out to hurt us. This knowing is the action of a loving King whose rule over the world is so complete and whose compassion for the world is so deep that he doesn't miss a thing.

And he never missed anything in the years gone by either. The psalm goes on:

For you created my inmost being;
  you knit me together in my mother's womb.
I praise you because I am fearfully and
 wonderfully made;
  your works are wonderful,
  I know that full well.
My frame was not hidden from you
  when I was made in the secret place,
  when I was woven together in the depths of the
  earth.
Your eyes saw my unformed body;
  all the days ordained for me were written in
  your book
  before one of them came to be.
How precious to me are your thoughts, God!
  How vast is the sum of them!
Were I to count them,
  they would outnumber the grains of sand—
  when I awake, I am still with you.
                                    (Psalm 139 v 13-18)

There is absolutely nothing in our pasts that has slipped his gaze. Even when we were a tiny cluster of cells, he was there—and not just inertly gazing at us as nature took its course but actively working in us, preciously making us who we are and putting in place good plans for our lives.

Take a moment to let that sink in. You are known. Perfectly. Profoundly. Purposefully. Known by the God who made you and loves you.

He didn't fall asleep and miss your painful childhood, or tune out the last time you cried. He is not unconcerned by your fears or uninvolved in your future. This God is with you. And he is inviting you to something special.

A little later in the Bible, Jesus utters these words:

> *Come to me, all you who are weary and burdened,*
> *and I will give you rest. Take my yoke upon you*
> *and learn from me, for I am gentle and humble in*
> *heart, and you will find rest for your souls. For*
> *my yoke is easy and my burden is light.*
>
> (Matthew 11 v 28-31)

We don't tend to talk about yokes much in the 21st-century West. It's an image with roots deeply embedded in agricultural practices which we have lost but which are still operating in many parts of the world today. A yoke is simply a wooden crosspiece that fits over the shoulders of two animals to ensure they keep walking together closely. This is also a picture that helps us understand the manner in which God is inviting us to walk with him.

The God who knows you wants you to know him. This is an invitation that covers more than just your anxiety, but he certainly cares about that too. He wants you to come to him. To walk so intimately with him that you move as one with him. It might sound a little strange to be "yoked" with God. It's certainly not about being tied up in a constrictive sense! Instead, this is an invitation to closeness. He wants us to be alongside him every moment of the day—with him in the lead and him taking most of the load.

He's invited you to walk through this life in relationship with him, and that means knowing you are never isolated but always understood. Always with a place—a person—to whom you can turn. Even in the small hours of the morning, there is a God to whom you can talk in prayer—openly, honestly, personally— about your pain.

And that all comes with the privilege of being part of his church—a whole community of fallible, messy people who live their lives in relationship with the one who loves them best.

All alone? Not according to Psalm 139. You couldn't be more loved or known.

6. LIE #2: EVERYTHING IS OUT OF CONTROL

We don't just experience events; we interpret them too. And the events that fuel our anxiety can nudge us towards an awful conclusion: that life is spiralling out of control.

Often, that is how it genuinely feels. What we wanted didn't happen, that person we loved let us down, the diagnosis we prayed for wasn't given or the future we longed for seems to be ebbing away. And, in the middle of it all, our minds are swirling with "what-ifs" and "maybes"—with our sense of being able to cope left in tatters. Surely this is evidence that life really is just random! With all the pressure and chaos, maybe you feel as if you are living in a whirlwind. Maybe you've concluded that the universe doesn't have any effective brakes at all...

Sometimes that sense of everything being out of control grows from a small challenge that gets "catastrophised" in our minds. That unwise comment you made, that error in your studies or work, gets blown out of all proportion, and you convince yourself that your career is over, your exam failed or your relationships irrevocably broken. For some, that may be what happened in your childhood—maybe you grew up receiving big consequences for small slips—and you've carried those thought processes into adulthood. For others, the tendency to catastrophise stems from what someone is telling you now—a boss whose standards are unattainable or a spouse whose abusive power leaves you cowering after the smallest mistake. Or possibly our own internal standards are miscalibrated; we expect perfection of ourselves, demanding that we respond to stress in ways that just aren't possible and seeing every minor "failure" as a disaster. Whatever the roots, the fruits are extreme: the smallest deviation from how we think life should be means our whole world seems to fall apart.

Sometimes the conviction that the world is spiralling is based on the sheer volume of our trials: a relative is dead, friends are deserting us, our nation is in turmoil and our health deteriorating fast. There really can be a catalogue of pain that exceeds what most people around us are having to endure. When that happens, there's a certain logical consistency in thinking that life is little more than a fast-flowing stream. If we're honest, it can be hard to see any order or overarching plan.

Of course, the more our anxiety whispers that everything is out of control, the more anxious we get! It's scary enough to have to face the tough stuff in our life, but to have to face it from a worldview that says there's no plan, no purpose, nothing to stop it getting worse—that's terrifying in the extreme. A vicious cycle develops as pain leads to fear, fear leads to hopelessness and hopelessness leads to even more worry and hurt. It's a cycle that can leave us feeling inert. Maybe, even as you read this, you're wondering how you can begin to face what lies ahead.

In the first book of the Bible, we meet a man called Joseph. To put it mildly, Joseph had reasons to wonder if life was spiralling out of control! He was born into a large family and one where the relationships were more than a little strained. His brothers hated him so deeply that they plotted to kill him and only relented when they saw an opportunity to make some cash. They sold him into slavery, and he was trafficked into a foreign land. There he went into the service of a man whose wife was not an upright or trustworthy woman. She made several passes at him and, when he rejected her advances, accused him of attempted rape. The result was that he was thrown into prison for a crime he didn't commit.

While locked up he made a couple of good friends. He knew one would be released and would return to the king's service quite soon, and so Joseph asked that friend to help expedite his own release. But his friend forgot. It wasn't until the most powerful man in the country needed some help that finally the light at the end of the tunnel began to shine through.

Joseph had a gift—with God's help he could interpret dreams—and so when the Pharaoh had a dream he didn't understand, Joseph was allowed out of prison to help. It was a step in the right direction, to be sure, but certainly not a relaxing day. There was Joseph, no longer incarcerated but now standing before a powerful king delivering a very unwelcome message: the significance of the dream was that the nation would soon face a life-threatening famine.

In the ancient world it was never safe to give kings bad news. But Joseph wasn't punished. Instead, he was given a job with more responsibility and pressure than most of us could even begin to imagine: to navigate an entire nation through the process of stockpiling resources that would help them survive the disaster to come. Oh, and then the brothers who had sold him into slavery turned up.

Can you imagine what Joseph's life must have been like? Can you begin to get your head around the catalogue of disasters—traumas—that he faced? All that uncertainty, a catalogue of betrayals, pressure beyond measure. In his shoes I think I would have felt more than a bit anxious! And yet, when he finally had a heart-to-heart with the brothers who had kick-started such a lifetime of uncertainty and pain, he said this:

> *You intended to harm me, but God intended it for good.*   *(Genesis 50 v 20)*

Joseph may have suffered greatly, but he was able to keep going because he knew something extraordinarily important. He knew that nothing in his life was out of control—even though it was out of *his* control.

There was plenty that was painful. There was a great deal that was evil and wrong. God certainly did not condone the way others treated Joseph. But over the painfulness of Joseph's experiences, there lay the perfection of God's plans—plans which meant that nothing of Joseph's horrors went to waste. God wove together the messy strands of Joseph's life in such a beautiful way that it culminated in this unpopular young man leading a nation through a crisis and saving the lives of many. What looked like chaos turned out to contain deep hope.

Our stories are not the same as Joseph's. It is highly unlikely that many of us will taste the depths of his suffering or the responsibility of his national leadership. But his life does point to an unchanging reality: our world is not out of control.

God says there is a plan—a plan that runs from before the beginning of time into eternity. This plan sees God gradually restoring the world to how it should be, as he brings people back into relationship with him. Yes, there is evil in the world too—evil that can wound us, floor us, make us wonder if life is worth living at all— but that evil can't derail God's good purposes to make all things new. One day the world will be beautiful again. And, in the meantime, all the tough things we are facing aren't evidence that life is spiralling, but milestones in the journey that the Lord is governing—a journey that *can* end somewhere good.

Hopefully, that is some encouragement in your anxiety—the truth that everything is all part of a good plan, not a random set of events. But there's even better on offer, too. God has made a promise to those who choose to follow him:

> *And we know that in all things God works for the good of those who love him, who have been called according to his purpose.* (Romans 8 v 28)

It's a cast-iron guarantee. In a specific, not just a general, sense, God is knitting together the tough things of the lives of those who love him—in ways that build us into ever more beautiful people. If you are following him, it's not just a case that life *can* end somewhere good, but that life *will* end somewhere good.

You won't be able to see that "good" every day. There will be moments when the pain shouts more loudly than the purpose. And, on those days, it's ok to lament—to cry out to God, to tell him how much it hurts, to ask for him to act and to plead for the strength to trust him in the interim. But, when you follow Jesus, there will come a time when you can look back over your life and see how God has woven together the different, difficult strands and brought about something wonderful. You will begin to glimpse the plans that he has had all along. You will gradually grow in confidence that nothing comes to us by chance but only ever from God's loving, fatherly hand.[8]

I don't know if you have ever watched a sculpture being crafted, a piece of fine art gradually being worked on or even just a gorgeous meal being cooked. There are aspects of the process that look messy or chaotic in the extreme, but the end result is beautiful. The mess is only a transitory stage through which the artist or chef passes in order to get to their goal. God offers to do the same in the lives of those who love him. He takes the pressured mess of our lives and crafts us into people who are increasingly as we are designed to be.

That's certainly how I view my story. There are parts of my life—abuse, addiction—that have seemed deeply out of control. The things coming at me, and the things coming out of me, have been deeply chaotic at times. Certainly, things have happened that, in and of themselves, were not good. I've frequently responded in ways that have made things worse. But God has worked through all that to make me into the person I am today: not perfect (not by a long shot!) but able to trust him more deeply, able to see him more clearly, able to have compassion and empathy for those around me, able to hold out hope to those who feel there is none. And he's not going to stop doing that exciting work. Would it have been easier if that tough stuff had never existed? Probably. But would I be the person I am today? Absolutely not!

This is the lens through which I invite you to see your own life too. Maybe there's been abuse, bullying, trauma and grief in your life, all of which have left you reeling in fear and pain. Perhaps you need to get help to stop abuse that is happening right now. Maybe there have been plenty of moments when you have acted in ways that have dragged yourself and others down, exacerbating your anxiety in the process. Maybe there's the regret of paths not taken and decisions not made. But God has invited you into a relationship with him. He can help you, too, learn to trust, discover hope and develop deeper friendships with those around you.

Is life out of control? Anxiety would have us believe so. But it's not true. When you put your faith in God, you can know not only that he is with you but also that he has plans for you. And his plans never backfire or fail.

7. LIE #3:
I HAVE NO WAY
OF KNOWING WHERE
TO TURN

I am not known for a good sense of direction. The basics of knowing whether to turn left or right at the end of the road frequently seem too hard for me to discern. You'd think that a map app might help, but it doesn't. Often, I simply don't know where to go.

In our anxiety we can feel equally at sea.

The anxious mind is often one that can be overwhelmed by options. Should I go to the party or stay home? If I go, will I make a fool of myself? Will I regret not staying away? But if I don't go, will people think me unsociable? Will I just end up crying alone?

Should I take on that extra responsibility, or will it be too much? Should I say yes to the job or stay in my current one? Would it be better to spend my money on this or that? Shall I take this decision now or wait to consult more people? If I just ignore it, maybe it will go away...

Or what about phobias? If I get on that plane, will it crash? Would it be wiser to cancel that trip? Or should I push through the pain? If I go, I'll end up embarrassing myself. I'll probably make it miserable for the other people around me. And then maybe they'll get fed up with me. Maybe I'll ruin the trip for everyone. But if I don't go, I'll be letting them down in a different way. They'll resent me messing up the plans. It's going to be a disaster whatever happens...

Sound familiar? Our minds can whir with the various alternatives. Questions abound as we try to guess what's best. We get floored as we wonder how the people around us will react. It can feel impossible to land on a decision. The simple reality is that often the anxious mind feels as if it doesn't know where to turn.

Sometimes we default to doing whatever we suspect will make those around us happy. But we can just end up living life as a puppet of what we imagine others might think or feel.

Sometimes we try to codify life into a series of rules about how we think things should be. In our heads we try to compile a comprehensive manual that sets out "If X happens, do Y". We may not choose to follow our own rules to the letter, but at least they're there, making us feel safe.

Indeed, some people try to treat the Bible a bit like that. They try to find a verse for every scenario they face and use it as guidance for both life's big and little decisions. But does that really work—is that really God's answer to people feeling lost?

The Bible does give some clear guidance for life. If you want to murder someone, don't! If you think that sleeping with your best friend's spouse is a good idea, it isn't! If you are choosing to work 14 hours a day, seven days a week, that won't end well—you need to rest! It does contain some big-picture principles for life.

There's also plenty of wisdom in the Bible—teaching on how some of the big-picture principles might look in everyday life. The book of Proverbs is particularly packed with this. The verses there remind us that laziness isn't going to enable you to do well at work, nagging isn't going to produce a happy home and, my own personal favourite, your neighbour isn't going to appreciate it if you are loud in the mornings, even if what you are doing is designed to help![9]

But the Bible isn't going to tell you whether to get on that plane, go to that party, apply for that job or pursue a specific form of cancer treatment. Christianity isn't a religion of rules. It doesn't list what to do on any given day.

The Bible does, however, show us a *person* who is willing to lead us through this confusing thing called life.

One of the best-known psalms in the Bible is Psalm 23. It's a song about a shepherd leading a sheep, and it begins like this:

> *The LORD is my shepherd, I lack nothing.*
> *He makes me lie down in green pastures,*
> *he leads me beside quiet waters,*
> *he refreshes my soul.*
> *He guides me along the right paths*
> *for his name's sake.*
> *Even though I walk*
> *through the darkest valley,*
> *I will fear no evil,*
> *for you are with me;*
> *your rod and your staff,*
> *they comfort me.* (Psalm 23 v 1-4)

This song reminds us that life is a real mix of lovely, restful things (green pastures), beautiful, pleasing things (quiet waters), and really hard things (the darkest valley). All of us, on our journey through life, will face a smattering of all of those. Some of us will spend a little longer in the darkest valley than others, but we could all do with someone to lead us through: a shepherd.

What is the role of that shepherd? To be a constant leader: providing a sense of direction, ensuring that the sheep has periods of moving forward and periods of rest, and making sure the sheep is provided with what it needs for the journey. The shepherd also protects the sheep both from its own stubborn ways (a staff was used to bring back sheep who wandered off) and from the dangers around (a rod was used more for warding off wolves and bears).

The song was originally written by a king who was describing his own personal relationship with God. It's also a song that can describe us—if we choose to follow our Shepherd.

The good news of the Bible isn't just that God is there and has a plan but that he is willing to lead us through that plan step by step. He's not an overlord looking to control us like robots but a wise Shepherd willing to walk ahead of us, providing everything we need to live life his way. It's a tender picture, a pastoral picture, that reminds us that there is someone we can follow through all the ups and downs of life.

What difference does that make? In the here-and-now, it brings a measure of peace. Those who accept Jesus as their Shepherd can know that he is leading, providing for and protecting them every step of the way. And when you grasp that, you can begin to understand that you don't need to be afraid anymore. The wolves and the bears may still come at you (God doesn't promise a problem-free life), and there may be occasions when you "wander off" by making decisions that are just so unhelpful (the Bible is eminently realistic about how wayward we can be), but through it all the Shepherd will keep moving us forward in the ways he knows to be best.

Later in the Bible, we find out that God gives a gift to all those who choose to follow him. It's the gift of himself—the Holy Spirit, who comes to live inside all those who believe in Jesus. He's more than our conscience. He's God. And it is his role to guide us, lead us, teach us and remind us just how wonderful our heavenly Father is.[10] Constant guidance from a shepherd, not just outside but inside.

When you are struggling, the Spirit can help you to pray. When you are confused the Spirit will help you make decisions that are wise. When you are paying too much attention to your own wayward thoughts—or to the unhelpful words of people around us—the Spirit can help us return our attention to God and hear what he has to say. The Spirit gives us the strength to live life counterculturally—putting our trust in God and persevering, even when life feels hard.

In the future, it gets even better. The last few verses of the psalm are a picture of a victory feast: a place of calm after the battle is over and there is no more fighting to be done. It's a picture of the end of time. There is a place where we can go, in the future, and live for ever in utter security:

> *You prepare a table before me*
> *in the presence of my enemies.*
> *You anoint my head with oil;*
> *my cup overflows.*
> *Surely your goodness and love will follow me*
> *all the days of my life,*
> *and I will dwell in the house of the* LORD
> *for ever.*   *(Psalm 23 v 5-6)*

Perfection is where the Shepherd is ultimately leading all of his sheep. God's "house" is a place of no more illness, discord, stress—or anxiety.

It can feel hard to imagine that when we're in the mud and mire of anxiety now. Perfection really does feel a million miles away. But the Bible is clear: that's where the Shepherd's journey goes. Far better than any holiday destination we can envisage, his end point is a place where we can enjoy him and his gifts in all their fullness: a place of abundance, a place—as one little girl in my church put it—where there will be "no more runny eyes".[11] And it's a place where, he has promised, things will never get broken again.

Floundering through life? Convinced there is no way of knowing where to turn? It doesn't have to be that way. There is a Shepherd willing to lead you, if you just follow him. And the destination couldn't be better.

8. LIE #4:
I CAN'T CARRY ON

There's something deeply exhausting about anxiety. Whether it's the relentlessness of having to battle out-of-control thoughts, the background tension of constantly scanning the world for risk or the simple reality that sleep can be elusive, being fearful of the future can leave us feeling as if we have nothing left to give.

Rather than bouncing out of bed in the morning, it can be a herculean task to emerge from the covers. Far from being keen to engage in work or social events, we may find that the day before us is a terrifying sight. Those social-media memes that encourage us to grasp the day and make every second count can feel like they're directed not just at different people but at a whole different species! Sometimes anxiety is a tiredness from which it feels like there is scant chance of escape.

Little wonder then that sometimes we want to give up the fight. Sometimes we get the urge to wave a white flag of surrender and say, "Enough. I just can't do this anymore."

For a few of us, that means genuinely wanting to end our lives. (If that is you right now, please, please phone your doctor, pastor, a helpline or, at least, a trusted friend who can walk with you through these desperate thoughts. It would be an absolute tragedy to act on them when there is so much hope for you.) For others, the sense of not being able to carry on is more rooted in a desire to withdraw from people, tasks, to-do lists or events. It's a drive to hide—in the hope that, if no one notices us, we might just be able to get through another day. For others still, the exhaustion may lead us to demand that others rally round and meet our needs. We genuinely believe that if the people around us would just get their act together, we might be able to cope.

There are flaws in such plans though. Whether we are pursuing hope in oblivion, hiding or demanding others' help, we will be disappointed.

That's not to say rest is wrong—far from it. It is good to take time out and have some proper down time. Arranging our days at a well-moderated pace, with regular breaks, is undoubtedly wise—there can be huge benefits to making changes to our routines. And it's not to suggest that we should never ask the people around us to do things differently; sometimes a shift in the dynamics or roles in the home can be pivotal in providing a context that is truly helpful for growth. But such strategies only address what's happening on the outside, without enabling us to grapple with what's going on inside.

So where do we find the strength to carry on?

Back in the early chapters of the Old Testament we meet a people whose history was steeped in pain. Joseph's family (who had grown to become the nation of Israel) found themselves in Egypt and deeply oppressed.[12] They were compelled to gather straw, make bricks and build whatever their masters demanded. They were worked relentlessly and ruthlessly and knew the awfulness of edicts that demanded their baby boys be put to death. They certainly knew the depths of brokenness that this life can bring.

They also, however, knew what it is to be rescued. God raised up leaders called Moses and Aaron. And the Lord sent ten plagues to afflict their oppressors. After the tenth plague, the Passover (where only those who trusted God's command to sacrifice a lamb escaped the terrible scourge of the death of the firstborn in every family), the people were allowed to leave slavery and start their journey to freedom.

It must have been an incredible series of events. They saw, first-hand, real, tangible evidence of God's presence, power and leadership. They moved from being slaves to being free. And yet they still struggled to keep going. They struggled because there was another facet of God's care that they had yet to grasp: his generous provision for his people day by day.

Just a month and a half after they had escaped from slavery, when hunger started to bite, they fell into all the same kinds of traps we fall into![13] They yearned for oblivion: "If only we had died". They demanded others sort things out: "They grumbled against Moses and Aaron", the Bible records. And, rather than engaging with their future, they wanted to retreat into their past. They even went as far as saying, "[In Egypt] we sat round pots of meat and ate all the food we wanted". (The whole slavery thing seems to have momentarily slipped their minds!) Life was better then, they thought—even though that couldn't have been further from the truth. It's easy to see the inadequacy of their responses to the (very real) stresses they were under. It's somewhat more sobering to acknowledge that we might just be the same.

How did God respond? Not in anger or exasperation. He simply gave them what they required—one day at a time.

On Mondays, they had to go out to gather the food they needed and eat it. On Tuesdays, out they went again.

Wednesdays too. Each day, they were given just what they required for that day (with a double portion on Fridays so they could have a proper rest the following day). If they tried to stock up, it went rotten. God didn't set up a system that enabled them to stockpile. The Lord didn't provide an environment in which they could be increasingly self-reliant. He enacted a method of provision that meant they had to rely on him as he provided for them day after day after day.

These days, life looks rather different. Most of us aren't in a desert. The majority of us aren't refugees from slavery, heading towards a new land (though that's not to say that there aren't many people in the world today who do have experiences like that). The supermarket is our most likely source of bread! But God's method of provision lives on. Each day he gives those who follow him exactly what they need to be able to live the day that he has set before them.

Trouble is, anxiety encourages us to look a long way ahead. We panic because we don't have what we need to be able to get through next week's job interview, next month's operation, next year's exam or some hypothetical crisis in the future. To which God says, *No, you don't—not yet—but you will when you get there. I'll give you what you need to live life in ways that honour me, at the time I know to be best. And you can trust me to keep that promise.*

It's worth saying that God's promise is to give us what we need, not to give us anything our crazy imaginations can dream up. I might dream I could one day be a pilot doing acrobatics in the sky (and just between you and me, even as someone scared of flying, I do sometimes watch aerial displays and think, "If only"!). But I can't hold God to fulfilling my fantasies. There's absolutely nothing in Scripture that gives me any reason to believe that one day I will be flying at over 600 mph, leaving a bright red trail in my wake! In the same way, he probably isn't going to equip us to work an 80-hour week without getting tired or to have a home where nothing is out of place! Workaholism and perfectionism are not things he equips us to pursue. He does equip us for faithfulness, though. And he never fails.

This offer of provision is open to anyone. The people in our Bible passage were weak (from decades of slavery), doubting (that they were heading anywhere good), grumpy (because life was hard) and just plain messy human beings (who couldn't even remember how horrible their past was!). They are proof that it's impossible to be so messed up that God wouldn't want to provide for you! But this promise comes with a clause: it was only those who followed God into the desert who got his daily provision. If they'd stayed behind in Egypt, they wouldn't have experienced his special care. God cares for all people in general ways, but the specific promise of daily provision is for those who have a personal relationship with the Lord.

Later in the Bible, Jesus makes an astonishing claim:

> *I am the bread of life. Whoever comes to me will*
> *never go hungry, and whoever believes in me will*
> *never be thirsty.* (John 6 v 35)

In other words: God doesn't just provide things to keep us going; he gives us the gift of himself. It is in Jesus that we have life, strength and all we need to persevere.

How does it work? Simply by getting up each morning and consciously engaging with our generous God. By looking in his word, the Bible, and feeding on the glorious truths that we find there—truths like the ones we have been looking at: God, right now, is present, sovereign, leading and providing in ways that do not fail. By talking to God and articulating exactly what we think we need but being willing to accept whatever he knows we need. By being willing to set aside dreams of how we want life to be and pursue the kind of life he wants for us, in the strength he provides. By combatting thoughts of being unequipped with the truth that—today—we *are* equipped. By reminding ourselves that, like a well-prepared hiker about to set out on a trek, we have all that we need to carry on.

Feeling "I can't do this anymore"? Try praying something like this: "Lord, if I am pursuing something that's not right, please let me stop. If I need rest, please help me take it. But if I am pursuing something that is good, please help me rely on you and know beyond any shadow of doubt that you are equipping me every step of the way."

9. LIE #5:
THIS IS ALL
MY FAULT

Guilt is fertile ground for anxiety to thrive.
Sometimes we're anxious because we genuinely have done something wrong. Our conscience is acutely aware of our harsh words, deceitful actions or careless treatment of others. We can be fearful of getting caught or having to face the consequences that our behaviour deserves. We might worry that others will shun us because of what we've done. Guilt stokes the fires of anxiety with a relentless passion.

Sometimes we're anxious because we assume we have done something wrong or probably will do something wrong in the future, even though there's no objective evidence that that's true. There have been many occasions when an anxious person has apologised profusely to me and I have been left confused, wondering how they could possibly think their actions have been in any way wrong! False guilt can be just as powerful a catalyst for anxiety as the real thing.

At other times we can be anxious about the things that have been done to us. It's not that we've objectively done anything bad, but the actions of others have left us feeling tainted or dirty or just plain wrong. Bullying and abuse often fall squarely into this kind of territory. The pain wasn't our fault, but it's left us feeling scared that others will see us as marred. Or we think, deep down, that maybe we really did deserve what happened to us. Shame, too, can enflame anxiety in the extreme.

When one or more of these aspects of guilt fuels our anxiety, our tendency can be to sink into either a wallow of self-pity ("I'm a horrible person—I deserve to feel this bad") or a frenzy of activity ("If I could just try harder to be better, I might be able to make these feelings go away"). Neither option works. Indeed, both are likely to induce far more anxiety than they take away.

The laws of the Bible are some of the most desperately misunderstood parts of Scripture. Often, we read them and think, "I need to keep these rules. If I do, God will accept me; if I don't, he'll hate me". Those of us who struggle lots with anxiety can easily become more ardent rule-keepers than most. There's something about the structure of order, discipline and measurables that plays right into our anxiety-ridden minds! And our view of God can easily become one of a hard taskmaster who needs to be pleased or even appeased. So we see rules like "Do not let any unwholesome talk come out of your mouths" or "Among you there must not be even a hint of sexual immorality" or "Remember the Sabbath by keeping it holy", our brains just scream "Fail! Fail! Fail!" We feel guilty and our anxiety levels rocket through the roof.[14]

Used correctly, however, the laws of the Bible can bring freedom in two very different ways.

First, the law passages help us discern what is and isn't wrong. For example, the Bible never says that earning money is wrong, so we don't need to feel guilty if we are comfortable; but it does tell us that the love of money is wrong and so there is a problem if we are fixated on getting rich.[15] The Bible never says that anger is wrong (in fact God frequently gets angry at injustice), but it does tell us that hurting others in our anger or leaving anger to fester is not ok and needs to be addressed.[16] God never judges the victims of abuse and says, "You are guilty" or encourages us to believe the negative things that others have spoken into our lives—he has compassion on the oppressed and says that the oppressors are the guilty ones.[17] So, rather than making up our own standards about whether we are guilty or not, we can look at God's standards and avoid labelling things that aren't wrong as wrong. We don't need to say sorry that our flat isn't pristine or that we're tired because we slept badly. We don't need to apologise for being sad when someone has died. We shouldn't feel guilty about struggling to enjoy intimacy with our spouse when we are still reeling from a sexual assault. Read carefully, the laws of the Bible can help us see where we have been misclassifying hardship as wrongdoing and feeling guilty as a result. That can be liberating in the extreme!

But, second, and even more importantly, the Bible can point us to a rather more lasting and satisfying solution to the type of guilt that is real than anything our anxiety has to offer.

Take an honest look at your life and you will see that there is quite a lot of evidence that you do have some things to feel guilty about. This is what the Bible calls being a sinner. That's not a popular word, I'll admit, but it is a Bible word and one that describes the basic problem of every human being: we have a deep-seated tendency to do things our way rather than God's way. Sin isn't simply an event like "I stole something once", nor is it a word reserved for terrorists, paedophiles and all those other criminals that society likes to set apart as being especially bad. No, the word "sinner" describes every human being who has ever thought, said or done anything that isn't what God would want.

And that's all of us. On one level, we all have things to feel guilty about!

"So I have good reasons to feel anxious then," you might be thinking. Well, not exactly. We are all guilty, but God doesn't want us to sit long-term in that guilt. He doesn't want us to experience the consequences of that guilt. Guilt is designed to be a fleeting state which pushes us towards asking God for full and complete forgiveness. And towards confidence that, because of Jesus, God will absolutely delight in giving us that forgiveness—washing us totally clean.

Imagine for a moment that you are wearing a white shirt. Every time you desire, say or do something that is not what God would want, you end up squirting yourself with ketchup or mustard. Messy, I know.

Now imagine that you have been wearing that same shirt your whole life. (Don't worry, it's stretched nicely as you've grown!) Can you visualise just how filthy that piece of clothing would be? For each of us the stain patterns would be different, but for all us, without exception, they would be awful. But don't despair…

Next, imagine a friend coming alongside you, a friend with a pristine shirt—not even a smudge of chilli sauce to be seen. What if they said to you, "Come on, let's swap—I'll take your shirt, you take mine"? It's the opportunity of a lifetime! A fresh start, with a new shirt. A chance to get rid of the past and to be clean, truly clean, for the first time ever.

That is the heart of the Christian message.

The gospel or "good news" of Christianity is that when Jesus, the Son of God, died on the cross and rose again 2,000 years ago, he was enacting a great swap. He was taking the punishment we deserve for our sins and offering us a brand new life—a life of forgiveness. He made it possible for us to pass all our wrongness to him and accept his "righteousness" (his rightness— his good standing with God) in its place.

People don't always think about Christianity like that. Sometimes people write it off as a religion of rules that is guilt-inducing—but it's designed to be guilt-removing. And God promises that everyone who is sorry for their sins and who asks for forgiveness will receive it (accepting that that's only possible through Jesus' work on the cross and knowing that it will mean living life differently in the future). As one of the New Testament letters says, we become people who can say:

> *In him we have redemption through his blood, the forgiveness of sins, in accordance with the riches of God's grace that he lavished on us.*
>
> *(Ephesians 1 v 7)*

And that word "lavished" really is right! God delights in pouring out forgiveness on anyone who turns to him.

What does that mean for our guilt-fuelled anxiety? It means that we don't need to feel guilty anymore. Even when we have genuinely messed up spectacularly, God says, *You're forgiven, you're clean, you're accepted and secure.* Once we've asked for and accepted his forgiveness, there are no grounds for seeing ourselves as guilty messes. We are his children: precious, clean and pure.

Of course, our human minds don't always manage to grasp this straight away. We may theoretically know that God has cleaned us, but part of us often suspects that maybe we're still a bit dirty really. Sometimes it takes time—and lots of reminders—to help the reality sink in. But his forgiveness of us truly is complete. He doesn't sit in heaven going, *I've forgiven all who have turned to me except...* No, he washes clean all who come to him in repentance and faith.

So, when our anxious minds whisper, "You idiot—you failure", how should we respond? We may need to say sorry if we have messed up. But we can also cling to God's verdict and say, "I'm forgiven, I'm free. I don't deserve it, but Jesus has made me clean. And that means I do not need to be ashamed, I don't need to earn God's favour, I don't have to flurry around trying to impress others or work myself into the ground. There's a big 'not guilty' verdict hanging over my life, and God is never going to change his mind about that."

10. LIE #6:
THERE'S NO HOPE
FOR ME

Can you really change?

Maybe there is a God who is present, sovereign, leading, equipping, forgiving and more—but will that make a tangible difference in your life?

I've lost count of the number of books I've read on anxiety. Sometimes when we struggle with something, we can have an insatiable appetite to understand it well. That's not wrong, but understanding our anxiety doesn't automatically transform it. We still need to change.

That's where a lot of people can come unstuck. We read about the techniques but think they're too hard. We read God's words but imagine they don't apply. We hear of the success stories but assume such tales can never be ours. We get trapped in our anxiety and assume there is no hope—not for someone like me.

Sometimes, such conclusions come after you have battled anxiety for many years and seen little improvement. Sometimes, they appear before you have even begun to fight—so ground down are you by the pain of your past. There are those who stagnate because they don't want to let go of the perfectionism, workaholism or rules-based living that God says is so damaging. There are others of us for whom the traumas of life just keep on coming; it's hard to recover from one before the next one hits. Still more people simply can't imagine what an anxiety-free life could be like; it's hard to walk towards something you can't visualise as even a remote possibility.

The exciting news of the Christian faith is that God loves to change people!

The Bible is packed full of passages that show us how both beginning to follow Jesus and continuing to follow Jesus can make a massive impact in our lives.

Take Zacchaeus.[18] This man was not one of life's upright characters! He was rich, by 1st-century standards, but his wealth had not been ethically earned; he was a collaborator with the occupying Roman forces and used his position as a tax collector to swindle a lot of people out of their hard-earned cash! It might be easy to think that a religious leader wouldn't want much to do with Zacchaeus and, indeed, most of the religious leaders of the day would have given him a very wide berth. But Jesus was different. When he spotted Zacchaeus sitting in a tree above the crowds, Jesus called to him and said he wanted to eat with him. We don't know exactly what Jesus said over the meal, but we do know that Zacchaeus was never the same again. The man who had stolen became generous; the man who had lied became honest. Meeting Jesus turned his life around.

It's the kind of story that can be echoed by many believers today.

A relationship with Jesus brings a freedom that nothing else can. It means that you no longer walk through life with a burden of guilt; you've been given a fresh start, and so you can live life very differently to the ways you have lived in the past. You no longer lack direction because you have a leader to follow and a sense of direction for your life that is good. You don't need to battle the painful facets of this life in your own strength because you have God within you, enabling you to persevere. You aren't dragged down by a mindset that shrieks that life is meaningless and out of control, but you know that every second of your life and every experience is steeped in great purpose. You aren't isolated but are in deep relationship with the one who made you, loves you and knows you more intimately than anyone else. It's a transformational relationship: one that is worth everything, one that is worth investigating more (and there is a list of books at the end to help you do that, if you'd like to).

Of course, we all lose sight of these wonderful benefits. Christians can *feel* guilty, directionless or afraid even when we know we have no need to. We continue to grow in our ability to trust these truths day by day. Nevertheless, these factors together are fertile ground for a life that is more grounded, more trusting, more persevering, more overflowing with hope.

It doesn't stop there. The Bible tells us that after we have started to follow Jesus, his Spirit will be at work in us, changing us to be more like him. Like a professional gardener gradually nurturing an overgrown garden back to beauty, God takes us on a lifetime's journey of being weeded, pruned, fed and watered—and he doesn't stop until we are just perfect. It's not a quick journey—he changes us slowly—but he never gives up. "He who began a good work in you will carry it on to completion until the day of Christ Jesus," the Bible says.[19]

Exciting though it is to focus on the fact that God is in the business of changing people, that doesn't mean there is nothing for us to do. Battling anxiety—like everything else in the Christian life—requires action on our part, not passivity. In relationship with God, and with other Christians, all believers are called to a life like this:

You were taught, with regard to your former way of life, to put off your old self, which is being corrupted by its deceitful desires; to be made new in the attitude of your minds; and to put on the new self, created to be like God in true righteousness and holiness. (Ephesians 4 v 22-24)

The Christian life is a daily call to leave old ways of thinking and behaving behind and, with our heads transformed by biblical truth, to pursue a more beautiful, trusting, God-reliant, people-loving life.

It may be helpful to think of your anxiety as a wall made up of individual bricks. Some of those bricks will be behavioural (for example, you drink or comfort-eat when you are scared—or retreat under your duvet); others of those bricks will be beliefs about yourself (I'm useless, I'm worthless) or beliefs about God (he doesn't care about me) and his world (everyone's a threat and social situations aren't safe); around those behaviours and beliefs will lurk experiences from your past (I've been bullied—I've been abandoned—I've been abused) and your present (I'm tired—my hormones have gone crazy—my boss is unbearable). Every brick plays its part in keeping your anxiety wall strong.

It's impossible to knock down this wall in one go. No one can say, "I'm going to stop being anxious today" and succeed. But you can begin to weaken the wall by replacing one brick at a time—taking off the old and replacing it with the new as your mind dwells on the beauty of God.

Maybe your anxiety wall looks something like this:

I comfort eat	I get panic attacks	I avoid socials	I retreat to my bed
I will never cope	I'm a failure	I'm a burden	I can't change now
God isn't going to help	People are fed up	Friends don't get it	People will wound me
My parents didn't love me	I was bullied at school	I've been rejected	I was told I'm ugly
I've just had a baby	Finances are tight	I'm exhausted	The weather is so hot

There are some things in that wall that can't be changed—the weather is beyond our control, the baby doesn't come with a returns policy—but most of the others can be addressed.

Some things can be "taken off" by reminding yourself of biblical truth and "putting on" new beliefs. If you are finding yourself repeatedly thinking, "I can't do this", it might help to look at a range of Bible passages that show us how wonderfully God equips his children. It may well be useful to listen to Christian friends as they tell their story of how God has helped them persevere. Memorising key verses (try Psalm 46 v 1—"God is our refuge and strength, an ever-present help in trouble") or writing them on post-it notes around the house can help you remember that God is active. Maybe you might even pick a favourite song to help you recall how much God is enabling you to carry on. As we actively do these things, our thinking begins to change; we no longer tell ourselves we can't do it, and become more and more convinced that, with Christ, we can.

Other bricks can be addressed by engaging more with God's offer of compassion and love and putting on the life of freedom he chooses to give. You may have been rejected by others, but you can remind yourself that God accepts you in his great love. You may still be reeling from being bullied, but you can hear God's words of comfort as you call out to him in your pain. God loves us to talk to him in prayer—and we don't need to be all sorted before we begin to speak. In the depths of your fears, you can pour out how you are feeling, knowing that he hears and will answer in the ways he knows to be best.

You can remember some of the wonderful ways in which the Bible describes God: as a fortress (where we can run when we are scared), a king (who is working all things together in his plans), a judge (who won't let the pain done go unpunished) and a father (who loves his children so very deeply). Talking to this compassionate God—and talking about his compassion with believing friends—can help you process the pain of the past. God's word reminds us that his compassion is active and he has plans to make things right.

Other strategies are more immediate and practical. You can ask God for self-control. You can ask others in his church to encourage you to "put on" a decision to pray and "take off" the habit of eating biscuits! You can enact grounding techniques when you feel panicky or ask a friend to stay by your side when you need help to engage socially.

It may sound quite a task! And battling anxiety is just that—a battle, at times. But it's not about summoning up the strength to defeat anxiety on your own. It is about taking hold of all the help that God is providing you with. You are called to fight, but you are never alone.

On one level it doesn't matter which brick we tackle first (though starting with beliefs and moving on to behaviour is a flow that many helpfully use). And there's no hurry; a lifetime of walking with Jesus gives us the time we need to slowly look at one brick at a time. It might take 3, 6, 12, or 18 months to replace that sense of "I'm a failure" with the truth that "I'm clean and full of purpose". Replacing those old thoughts with new ones may take may hours of reading Bible passages that remind us that Jesus has forgiven us, has prepared good works for us to do and doesn't reject us. We may need to catch those "I'm a failure" thoughts multiple times a day and—every time—say, "Sorry, no—that's not true, is it? Let me focus again, Lord, on what you say." It might involve many hours of prayer where we pour out our hearts to God, saying, "But I feel like a failure... how will I ever get to the point of believing what you proclaim?" And it will certainly involve gentle friends looking us in the eye and asking, "Failure? Really? Is that who you are in Christ?"

It's not a race. You will mess up more than once. But gradually that brick will loosen, come out and be replaced by something far better.

Doomed to stay the same? Not in the slightest! Brick by brick, you discover there is hope for people like you, and anxiety's grip begins to wane.

POSTSCRIPT

Maybe the question on your lips is: "So can I ever be completely free of anxiety?"

To which the answer is a resounding "Yes! But..."

The Bible story tells us that anyone who follows Jesus has a happy ending to their life. In the future, there will be a new heaven and a new earth, and they will be so perfect that there will be neither any anxiety nor any bad experiences that could trigger anxiety. In the next life, believers will be invited to live with the one they believe in for eternity. As we saw earlier, the Bible describes that like this:

> Look! God's dwelling-place is now among the
> people, and he will dwell with them. They will
> be his people, and God himself will be with them
> and be their God. "He will wipe every tear from
> their eyes. There will be no more death," or
> mourning or crying or pain, for the old order of
> things has passed away.   (Revelation 21 v 3-4)

It really is an astonishing future to look forward to. And a guaranteed worry-free zone!

But before then? Will there be respite in the here-and-now?

As we put our faith in him and continue to grow in that faith, our struggles with anxiety will change.

For some of us, that will mean conquering anxiety completely. It would be unrealistic to expect to avoid all forms of stress in this broken world, but there certainly can be freedom from the crippling effects we battle today.

Others of us will see our anxiety decrease substantially as we trust God more and enjoy that lifetime journey of taking off our old self and putting on the new. Maybe it won't completely go, but there will come a time when we can look back and revel in how much we have changed. It genuinely is possible to become more trusting, more secure, more confident in the promises of God.

For a few, anxiety will remain a significant struggle— God never promises to take away the hard things in this life, and so we can't assume that he will—but there is hope here too. The anxiety may still persist but there's no walking the path of an anxious life alone. Both God and his people will be around you—loving you, encouraging you, nourishing you, enabling you to persevere.

And whichever of these categories you fall into, you can fuel your progress. You can turn to God in trust through Bible reading, prayer and going regularly to church. You can turn to others in trust—both believers at church who can spur you on in your journey and medical professionals who have expertise to help. You can turn to other resources—whether that's a bigger book on anxiety or one that simply helps you understand God more.

Most important, however, is to hear the glorious invitation God is holding out right here and now. He reminds us that we don't have to journey alone. Or in our own strength. Or without a sense of direction. Or while carrying burdens of guilt. God offers an alternative in all those areas and more. As Jesus gently said to those who came to him:

> *Do not worry about your life, what you will eat or drink; or about your body, what you will wear. Is not life more than food, and the body more than clothes? Look at the birds of the air; they do not sow or reap or store away in barns, and yet your heavenly Father feeds them. Are you not much more valuable than they? Can any one of you by worrying add a single hour to your life? ... But seek first his kingdom and his righteousness, and all these things will be given to you as well.*
>
> *(Matthew 6 v 25-27, 33)*

FURTHER READING

To help with your anxiety

A Small Book for the Anxious Heart by Edward Welch (New Growth Press, 2019)

Down, Not Out by Chris Cipollone (The Good Book Company, 2018)

Living Without Worry by Tim Lane (The Good Book Company, 2015)

Real Change by Andrew Nicholls and Helen Thorne (New Growth Press, 2018)

Running Scared by Edward Welch (Evangelical Press, 2007)

To help you find out more about Christianity

Finding More by Rico Tice and Rachel Jones (The Good Book Company, 2019)

If You Could Ask God One Question by Barry Cooper and Paul Williams (The Good Book Company, 2008)

King's Cross by Timothy Keller (Hodder and Stoughton, 2011)

To help you get to know God better

Basic Christianity by John Stott (IVP, 2013)

Enjoying God by Tim Chester (The Good Book Company, 2018)

Gentle and Lowly by Dane Ortlund (Crossway, 2020)

Need to Know by Gary Millar (The Good Book Company, 2020)

NOTES

[1] www.nhs.uk/conditions/generalised-anxiety-disorder (accessed 26 Oct. 2020).

[2] www.mind.org.uk/information-support/types-of-mental-health-problems/statistics-and-facts-about-mental-health/how-common-are-mental-health-problems (accessed 26 Oct. 2020).

[3] You can find it in the Gospel of John, chapter 4.

[4] Psalm 94 v 19.

[5] Philippians 2 v 28.

[6] 1 Peter 5 v 7.

[7] Genesis 2 v 4-25.

[8] Heidelberg Catechism, question 27.

[9] Proverbs 20 v 4; 21 v 19; 27 v 14.

[10] John 14 v 26.

[11] Thanks, Emilia—you're great!

[12] Exodus 1.

[13] Exodus 16 v 1-3.

[14] Ephesians 4 v 29; 5 v 3; Exodus 20 v 8.

[15] 1 Timothy 6 v 10.

[16] Ephesians 4 v 26-27.

[17] Psalm 9 v 15-18.

[18] Luke 19 v 1-10.

[19] Philippians 1 v 6.

ACKNOWLEDGEMENTS

It's always a privilege to write a book, but it's never something that can be accomplished alone. So, a big thank you to:

- All those people who have shared their stories of anxiety with me—your honesty has been humbling and your willingness to show me how you have persevered through hardships has been an absolute inspiration.

- My colleagues at Biblical Counselling UK—your prayerful support has been such an encouragement.

- The incredible staff at The Good Book Company, especially Katy, Carl and André—your patient wisdom has been a joy.

- Those friends who read the manuscript and helped me think more clearly—Tom, Steve, your comments were invaluable.

- And a special thank you to all those who help me keep my sights on Jesus when I feel afraid—not least the wonderful staff at Dundonald Church. Eyes up!

Most of us wonder: is there something more to life?

Finding More tells the stories of eleven people who asked that question, and found the answer.

These fascinating life stories introduce you to people from all kinds of backgrounds who became Christians when they encountered the only One who gives us more: Jesus Christ. As their stories unfold, you'll be shown who Jesus is, why he came, and what it means to follow him.

thegoodbook.com/finding-more
thegoodbook.co.uk/finding-more

Whether you have experienced mental illness yourself, or want to understand depression and anxiety to care for somebody you love, this book provides a personal and theologically-thoughtful reflection on the challenges facing Christians in this area.

thegoodbook.com/down-not-out
thegoodbook.co.uk/down-not-out

thegoodbook
COMPANY

Thanks for reading this book. We hope you enjoyed it, and found it helpful.

Most people want to find answers to the big questions of life: Who are we? Why are we here? How should we live? But for many valid reasons we are often unable to find the time or the right space to think positively and carefully about them.

Perhaps you have questions that you need an answer for. Perhaps you have met Christians who have seemed unsympathetic or incomprehensible. Or maybe you are someone who has grown up believing, but need help to make things a little clearer.

At The Good Book Company, we're passionate about producing materials that help people of all ages and stages understand the heart of the Christian message, which is found in the pages of the Bible.

Whoever you are, and wherever you are at when it comes to these big questions, we hope we can help. As a publisher we want to help you look at the good book that is the Bible because we're convinced that as we meet the person who stands at its heart—Jesus Christ—we find the clearest answers to our biggest questions.

Visit our website to discover the range of books, videos and other resources we produce, or visit our partner site www.christianityexplored.org for a clear explanation of who Jesus is and why he came.

Thanks again for reading,

Your friends at The Good Book Company

thegoodbook.com | thegoodbook.co.uk
thegoodbook.com.au | thegoodbook.co.nz | thegoodbook.co.in

WWW.CHRISTIANITYEXPLORED.ORG

Our partner site is a great place to explore the Christian faith, with powerful testimonies and answers to difficult questions.